We Overcome All Things
In Our Father's Hands

Myeisha Johnson

WESTBOW
PRESS
A DIVISION OF THOMAS NELSON

WestBow Press books may be ordered through booksellers or by contacting:

WestBow Press
A Division of Thomas Nelson
1663 Liberty Drive
Bloomington, IN 47403
www.westbowpress.com
1-(866) 928-1240

Because of the dynamic nature of the Internet, any web addresses or links contained in this book may have changed since publication and may no longer be valid. The views expressed in this work are solely those of the author and do not necessarily reflect the views of the publisher, and the publisher hereby disclaims any responsibility for them.

Any people depicted in stock imagery provided by Thinkstock are models, and such images are being used for illustrative purposes only.

Certain stock imagery © Thinkstock.

ISBN: 978-1-4497-1513-7 (sc)
ISBN: 978-1-4497-1514-4 (e)

Library of Congress Control Number: 2011926674

Printed in the United States of America

WestBow Press rev. date: 4/8/2011

I Dedicate This Book To:

My Mother and Children
Thank you for all of your love and support!

Contents

Introduction

*I*f you are interested in finally reading a book that is not afraid to confront the topics that most people deal with in life, but avoid in conversation, then you have found the right book. In this book, you will find healing from hurts such as abandonment, rape, low self-esteem, physical abuse, and more. As an overcomer of sexual, emotional, verbal, and physical abuse, I am well acquainted with what pain and fear feels like. There's the pain of knowing what is happening to you is wrong, and the fear of telling someone. The pain of feeling like everything wrong around you is your fault, and the fear of taking your own life. There is also the pain of thinking that you will be like this forever, and the fear that everyone around you will notice your differences.

When reading this book you will be able to see life as I did before I developed a relationship with Christ, and compare it to my life today. I want you to feel assured in knowing that 1. You don't walk alone in how you feel and portray life, 2. Our Lord God brings abundant life and not death, and 3. You can overcome every hurt, habit, and hang-up that has you tied down, and has kept you from having life's best.

Victory lies within our grasp, and our dreams are never out of reach. And remember, **You are an overcomer because Jesus has overcome the world!** God Bless You!

PART ONE

We Overcome Mediocrity
We Overcome Suicide
We Overcome Molestation
We Overcome Death
We Overcome the Enemy
We Overcome Stumbling Blocks
We Overcome Betrayal
We Overcome Autonomy

We Overcome Mediocrity

And the LORD shall make thee plenteous in goods, in the fruit of thy body, and in the fruit of thy cattle, and in the fruit of thy ground, in the land which the LORD sware unto thy fathers to give thee.

Deuteronomy 28:11

The Struggles of Life

It was once hard to believe that one day I'd be out on my own.
I use to be scared and wish to be younger,
but now I wish to be alone.
Deep in my heart I know I still love, but
on the outside it's hard to see.
I often wonder what my life would be like three
years from now and who will be here for me.
People have changed and time steadily goes by as
I wait for the result of my accomplishments.
I can see myself in a normal occupation with enough
financial support to pay off my human debts.
Most of my future is blurry and seems out
of reach because of inexperience.
I was once told I would not go far and would
settle for less because of defiance.
Who will I be and where will I be, is what
I ask myself from day to day.
I do have other responsibilities to tend to,
but they don't in any way relay.
Each day I look out of my window at all nature that is truly free.
Birds, squirrels, trees, and flowers all
bring me peace and harmony.
Now I sit here and write to put all of
my frustrations out on paper.
I wish and I hope everything will work out for the better.

There Ain't No More Struggling

It doesn't hurt as much, anymore, to
think of my unforgettable past.
How I would run to so many happy faces, only to
find a depressing love that would not last.
Thank God for my Jesus, who lifted me from my lowest point.
For he cleaned me up, gave me a new suite, and, best
of all, promised that our lives could be joint.

I remember what it felt like not to be able to smile.
Your true desire is to be gracefully and wonderfully
free, but every tormenting and narcissistic issue
pulls you back into its dirty waste pile.
Thank God for my Deliver that is the only one
that could pay that remarkable price for me.
For He hung his head with authority, He gave up the
ghost attaining might, and He rose, He rose, He rose,
with all power and all glory brimmed in His hands.

Sometimes I think of what is was like to always fail.
No matter whom you do it for, or how well you did
it, there was just no room for you to excel.
But thank God for my Armor and Shield
who so beautifully sits on high.
Yes! He is the only one I choose to please now, and
it is just by having faith and drawing him nigh.

As I look at my new and transformed life through the eyes
of my Jesus there is one thing that is so plain to see.
My fathers loving grace and His tender, warm mercy are
both endless and always abounded plentiful towards me.

Do I deserve any of it? Am I even worthy of His endless love?
Or am I perfect, someone special, or even
thought of as highly as a dove?

Nope! None of these things do I deserve, or have I
earned, and certainly did not make possible.
But it is my God who is mighty in me that makes me well
deserving, make me worth all the love he supplies, makes
me oh so perfect, makes me someone special, garments
me with high status and a new reputation, and allows me
to do the unbelievably and inconceivably impossible.

May all honor and praise be to God, for
He inhabits me and I, Him!
For with each small and great battle we win, I glisten
more and more as His gorgeous and precious gem.

We Overcome Mediocrity: Prayer

Heavenly Father, in the name of Jesus, I humbly come before you. I want you to know that I appreciate you for who you are, and thank you for opening my eyes to my deadly way of thinking and my defeated way of living.

Right now Father I use the measure of faith you have given me and apply Deuteronomy 28:11-13 to my life where you promised me abundant prosperity when I choose to serve you with my whole heart. So, I thank you right now in advance that I am no longer at the bottom, but at the top. I thank you in advance that I lend to many, and borrow from no one. I thank you for blessing the work of my hands, and that every other scripture which promises prosperity and abundant living applies to me. In Jesus name I pray. Amen.

We Overcome Mediocrity:
My Thoughts

_____

_____

_____

_____

_____

_____

_____

_____

_____

_____

_____

_____

We Overcome Suicide

The thief cometh not, but for to steal, and to kill, and to destroy: I am come that they might have life, and that they might have it more abundantly.

John 10:10

How I Wish It Were Time

Day in day out, it is the same old thing.
It hurts waking up knowing what today will bring.
Even though I try to make things better,
everything is still the same.
When everything is gone and the day is
gone, I am the one left to blame.

Oh, how I wish it were time.

I constantly ask myself, why try to succeed.
Especially, when knowing, that this world is made
up of nothing except genders and creeds.
As I picture myself in society, nothing prevails.
I was put here for a reason, but damned by everyone to fail.

Oh, how I wish it were time!

A Change of Heart

At one time, I thought I was truly ready to die.

It hurt so much to know that all of my painful life;
I had been living a great exhausting lie.

But, now I see how remarkably wonderful life can be.

And how easy it becomes with the Father beside me.

We Overcome Suicide:
Prayer

Oh, Heavenly Father! I bless you, praise you, and love you for all that you are to me. I thank you for sending Jesus to die for my sins and shortcomings. And, I thank you that as you said in John 10:10 that you also sent Jesus to give a full, abundant life that I can enjoy, and be prosperous in. Thank you Lord that now that I have chosen to give you full control of my life, everything that Jesus came and died for applies to me. I receive it right now in Jesus name, and I choose to live and not die. I thank you for the overflow of spiritual blessings that is about to pour into my life because I have made is awesome choice. In Jesus name, Amen!

We Overcome Suicide:
My Thoughts

We Overcome Molestation

For we have not an high priest which cannot be touched with the feeling of our infirmities; but was in all points tempted like as we are, yet without sin.

Hebrews 4:15

Innocence

Away at play, my brother and I were one day.
Because of all the happiness in the room, one
wouldn't think things would go this way.
But strangely enough, my innocence was stolen.
And along with it, my heart was molded.
It is written that what you do to others will
come back to you just as hard.
Sadly, to my surprise, it was my closest loved
one who was feathered and tarred.
Why do things happen the way they do.
I guess it's because we need a reason to start new.

Who Knows the Truth

I have come to know the many ways a child
can be robbed of their innocence.
All it takes is a man's foul manner and
a young woman's ignorance.
How foolish and close-minded love can make a woman in need.
No advice or even the plain truth will she pay heed.
What about the children?
Do they hold any importance?
When making a decision, never do we
consult our children in the pretence.
Really it is funny how we call ourselves children of God
Always so quick to swear, boast, and extend the rod.
Then we question why our lives are so corrupt.
The answer is simple; it is because of the plan we disrupt.
So what do we do?
How do we bring about change?
We must start with ourselves before all can rearrange.
The struggle will be hard, and the enemy count will be great.
But those who hate, harm, and bring
about horror seal their own fate.
All I have is one thing to say.
The book of life is what Jesus will hold high on judgment day.
Will you be ready?
Or will you have to stay?
It is all up to you, and your willingness to obey.

We Overcome Molestation:
Prayer

Sweet, Sweet Father of Heaven. Every time I think of your mercy toward me, and how you have been with me through everything I have endured in my life tears of joy begin to fall. In Hebrews 4:15 and 16, you remind me that you are concerned with the things that concern me. You have always been able to understand the pain I feel from a broken heart and spirit.

I thank you for always being available for me, and loving me as no one ever has. I come to you asking you to remove the pain that remains in my heart. I also ask that you would allow me to forgive those involved in taking advantage of me, and show me Lord that it was not my fault. Help me to overcome the thoughts I have, and remove the fear of being hurt again. In Jesus name I pray. Amen.

We Overcome Molestation:
My Thoughts

_____

_____

_____

_____

_____

_____

_____

_____

_____

_____

_____

_____

_____

_____

We Overcome Death

For God hath not appointed us to wrath, but to obtain salvation by our Lord Jesus Christ, Who died for us, that, whether we wake or sleep, we should live together with him

I Thessalonians 5:9-10

My Great Loss

One cold December night, in the land of dreams, I am awoken by a terrifying scream.

I run into my mother's room, and there first I see, my mother, and then my baby brother lying cold and blue.

I ask my mother what to do.

"Call you grandmother. Tell her it is an emergency. From there she will know what to do!"

I began to cry not know what to think.

Everything is happening so fast I can hardly blink.

"Grandma! Grandma! Get over here quick! Something is wrong with Jr. I think he is sick!"

What seemed like eternity were only minutes as we waited for help to come.

Not knowing what is happening, I feel so dumb.

My mother continually blows air into his mouth, hoping for any movement.

But not a hit, kick, or cry came from him at any moment.

"Hello ma'am, we got here as soon as we can. Have you tried CPR?" (They tried it again)

"Myeisha let your grandmother in!"

I did not want to, because I'd miss everything then.

When I turned around to see what was happening next.

The man had taken a shocker to his chest.

"We have a pulse, but it is very weak.

We should get him to the hospital before we loose the heartbeat!"

"Go and pack you and your brother some clothes," my grandmother said.

I did so quickly, and snatched my brother out of bed.

We waited and waited for Mommy to come back.

My Grandmother rocked us back and forth as we cried for the mother that we lacked.

All of a sudden, I heard the phone ring.

It was my mother only with sad news to bring.

"Your brother is gone. He's in heaven now," my grandmother gently explained.

"What so you mean he's gone? Is he never coming back? Why did he go?" I angry exclaimed.

Family and loved ones came from many of places.

But because of confusion and hurt, I couldn't stand to see their faces.

Everyone close I put to blame.

Not understanding death, I couldn't be tamed.

And doctor after doctor could not help me see.

They took him away, and now won't let me be.

Prayer is what truly got me through.

And with a new baby sister, I could start new.

It is Worth the Cost

Thank you Lord for being so wonderful to me.
You have taken what everyone thought to be tainted,
and molded it into what you intended it to be.

I am so blessed to be able to look back at
my life, and not cry anymore.
I love you, praise and worship you, and it is only you I adore.

I am forever grateful, and what you to
use me however you please.
Confidently I know that wherever you send
me, you will provide a holy ease.

I know there will be things that I fear, and may not want to do.
But I am comforted in knowing I am sufficient
in your sufficiency, and that you will give
me strength and guide me though.

Amen.

We Overcome Death:
Prayer

Sweet, Sweet Father of Heaven; How I adore you. I thank you for my life, and your word that you have given me to guide me through it. I thank you Lord that through the pain I feel of losing my loved one you comfort me. Even when I wasn't aware of your presence in my life, you gave me the strength to carry on despite the pain.

In 1 Thessalonians 5:9-10 you said Jesus died for the world so that whether we are dead or alive we may live together with him. I thank you Lord for giving me the chance to live together with you despite how badly I have messed up in the past.

Lord I pray that if my loved one died not choose to live with you on the Earth that I would not blame myself or others for their choice. I pray that I would forgive myself, and others for the role we might have played in their death, and confess that I will no longer feel guilty or cause myself anymore pain. Thank you in advance for freeing me from the bondage of guilt and shame. In Jesus name I pray, Amen.

We Overcome Death:
My Thoughts

We Overcome the Enemy

Ye are of God, little children, and have overcome them: because greater is he that is in you, than he that is in the world.

1 John 4:4

Weeping Willow

Weeping Willow
It's another night that I clench my pillow.
If I could relate to anything it would be a weeping willow.
The root of it would be my soul, the fallen leaves
would be the broken pieces of my heart, and the
branches are my arms trying to reach out for Him.
As the leaves of my tree continue to fall, I say to myself
that I can't make it because of he, she, and them.

Look at me! I have not one material thing to offer.
It is hard to accept that as long as my spiritual
life stays beautiful I will not suffer.

Intelligent and beautiful, this I am.
Never would I negotiate who I am for any man.
So why does it feel as if I can't do nothing right.
For my voice, independence, and God do I fight!

I know that in the end there will be
only a hand full left standing.
And though I can't see it; I can feel my father
restoring my root and gathering my leaves.
It is because of this to God my heart does sing.

Weep No More, We Are Free!

You thought you had me, but see I was born to win.
How dare you try to kill me with my own father's sin!
Oh Yeah! I am enjoying the thought of you watching
me rise out of the ashes and through the smoke.
For I am fully refurbished, and breathing
the overcoming breath of hope.
No more wondering, no more crying through the night.
No more fear that I would take my own
life before the next daylight.
I am free, I'm free, I'm free I say!
I fight this fight with peace day by day!
I can't be overtaken with ease anymore!
For I've tasted the King, and I see his arms
stretched out thru that open door!
I have no reason to cry or look back to Egypt.
Cause I can see all those who were above
me, below me, being whipped.
And yet I still pray for the fate of their souls.
Please, God, Please make that same old stupid stuff seem old!
And give them a new life without fault or blemish.
Because I can't stand to see them being
carried away as the world diminishes.

I hear a voice speaking so gently to my heart.
"Daughter I love you and have set you apart.
Above these beautiful clouds you will soar.
And with my word, as a fierce lion, you shall roar.
And I will give you all the desires of your heart.
And the path I have given you please don't fear it as you start.
And no matter how hard it gets don't take your eyes off me.
Always remember daughter I have given you the victory.
Now go in peace, sweet one, as I have ordered your steps.
And know that I have not ever made a
promise that I have not kept."

Can you hear him, for he speaks to you too?
He sent me here to tell you, "Daughter/Son I love you!"
Don't shut up your eyes or cover you ears.
Don't trust what you know deep down inside are lies and fears.
For you're free, you're free, you're free he exclaims.
Now arise! For you have been cleansed
of all foul odors and stains!
Amen!

We Overcome the Enemy:
Prayer

Father God, in Jesus name, I am grateful that you have all power in Heaven and Earth. I thank you so much for sacrificing your son's life that I may not only have everlasting life, but also so I would have power over the devil.

I now exercise this power you have placed within me, and command the devil to take his hand off of my life, my money, my physical body, my mind and thoughts, and my family. I cancel every mission that the devil has planned to try and destroy my life in the name of Jesus.

I command for the promises of your word to be applied to my life. Lord, I give you permission to manifest your plan, and blessings for my life. Thank you in advance for the great spiritual and material changes that about to take place in my life. In Jesus name I pray, Amen.

We Overcome the Enemy: My Thoughts

We Overcome Stumbling Blocks

Wherefore seeing we also are compassed about with so great a cloud of witnesses, let us lay aside every weight, and the sin which doth so easily beset us, and let us run with patience the race that is set before us

Hebrews 12:1

Pennies

Pennies, pennies, shinny little coins.
Can you believe they can cause pain down in your loins?
Pennies, pennies, worthless as they may seem.
Nightmares of them do I have when I dream.

I Am On My Way!

There are so many nights I have dreamed of terror and pain.
Although I have forgiven everyone involved,
there is still one that brings tears of rain.

It always begins simple, seeing my sibling and I getting
useless pennies from the top of the refrigerator.
We race outside to the ice cream truck to buy 3-cent
candy, and eat most, but save some for later.

Happy we seem, but suddenly the mood changes
and things become extremely dark.
Fear overtakes us as a silent room throbs of beating hearts.

The darkness grows heavier and heavier
and draws closer and closer.
We scatter to avoid fierce blows from an
electrical cord that strikes as a bulldozer.

For seconds I feel safe, but know I need to prepare for my fate.
I hear the screams of my sibling as he is
devoured by anger and hate.

As the dark draws near to me, I run
away taking blows to my back.

My escape ends when I am cornered in a room
between an ironing board and it's rack.

My head is being kicked against the wall
as I beg for the pain to end.
Blood came from my nose and face, and, as I began to lose
consciousness, the satisfaction intended was gained.

Being able to share your hurts with God and someone you trust is vital to your recovery process. Once you have exposed your weaknesses openly, the devil can no longer use them to hurt you. I thank God for you, and for the great things he has begun to do in your life. Please continue to be encouraged, and know that I am celebrating with you as you overcome.

We Overcome Stumbling Blocks: Prayer

Father God, in Jesus name, I thank you for every victory you have given me in my life. I acknowledge that it is you, God, who is changing the way I see others, and myself and I appreciate it.

I pray Lord that you would send a mature child of God, of my same gender, into my life that I can share my victories and shortcomings with. I ask that this person would have listening ears, know your word and promises, and have a heart to please you as they help me.

I also pray that you would begin to open my eyes to recognize this person when they come across my path. May I will be willing to show my weaknesses, and receive the guidance that you have given them to give me. I thank you in advance for this person, and I ask that you would begin to bless them now as you prepare their heart for this great task. Thank you in advance for not allowing my past and the people involved in it to be a stumbling block any longer.

I love you, and it's in Jesus name I pray, Amen.

We Overcome Stumbling Blocks:
My Thoughts:

_____

_____

_____

_____

_____

_____

_____

_____

_____

_____

_____

We Overcome Betrayal

Now he that betrayed him gave them a sign, saying, Whomsoever I shall kiss, that same is he: hold him fast.

Mathew 26:48

Time and Time Again

Time and time again you said you'd be there
To comfort me in sorrow and love me beyond compare
Through all of my setbacks you said you'd be by my side
To lift me up and restore my pride
But when all else failed you weren't there
And now I'm alone, and deep in despair

Time and time again you promised things would change
For the worst was for the best, and will make all rearrange
In my time of need you said you'd provide
For I will always come first, and never collide
But when all else failed you were no where to be found
And now I've stumbled, and wonder around

Time and time again you lied of your progress
Knowing you have accomplished nothing, and settled for less
Because of my morals and values I stood by you
I was bold, strong, and saw everything through
But when all else failed I turned to another
And now I am happy, and my heart belongs to another

My True Love

The love of my life can compare to no other.
He is one of wisdom, honesty and sees no particular color.

The love of my life is high and mighty.
He is one of courage, strength, and takes
nothing about me lightly.

The love of my life has the power to do anything.
He is one of blessings, forgiveness, and will
secure anyone under His wing.

The love of my life was once of the flesh, but is no longer.
He is one of completeness, purity, and for
material things He'll never hunger.

The love of my life will stand His ground until the very end.
He is one of His word, His people, and for all of those
who love Him; He'll be a father and a true friend.

Thank you Father for the love that I can never repay!

We Overcome Betrayal: Prayer

Heavenly Father, in Jesus name, I exalt you for who you are. I praise you for the awesome price that you paid at Calvary for my sins, and the sins of the world. Thank you for being willing to be betrayed, whipped, beaten, spat upon, nailed to a cross that you carried, and more just for me so that I could choose to have a life free of grief and sorrow.

Father, I present before you the pain within my heart that has been caused by strangers, friends, and loved ones. I ask that you would allow me to be able to forgive those who have caused me pain, and heal my broken heart. Show me your unfailing love, and fill my every void and need. I want to stop looking for love in all the wrong places, people, and things. Create in me a new heart so that I can serve you and love you with my whole heart, mind, and spirit. In Jesus name I pray, Amen.

We Overcome Betrayal:
My Thoughts

_____

_____

_____

_____

_____

_____

_____

_____

_____

_____

_____

_____

_____

Overcome Autonomy

I will run the way of thy commandments, when thou shalt enlarge my heart.

Psalm 119:32 (Amplified)

Run

Run, Run, Run as the wind.
Up over hills and thru the bends.
As fast as you can, and as strong as you may.
No time for chat, No time for play.

Run, Run, Run as the sea.
Out of great rivers where the next land may be.
Always on track, never loose your course.
No time for sorrow, No time for remorse

Save Me!

I have heard of the great things you do,
But I don't really know your name.

I have seen you in my dreams,
But wonder if in person you will look the same.

Lord, I believe you died on the cross for my sin and my shame,
Jesus I know that you rose from the
grave with victory I proclaim!

Please enter into my life, and give me a brand new start.
I realize I can't change my past or fix myself,
and I need a brand new heart.

I thank you in advance for the change in me.
Faithful and humble to you I will always be.

Amen.

We Overcome Autonomy:
Prayer

Dear Heavenly Father, I humbly come before you and give you the honor that you are worthy of. Lord, today I place my whole life into your hands. I am tired of trying to do things my own way, and running away from situations when they become too hard to bare. Bring order and peace to my life, and make your voice clearer to me so that I can hear you when I am ready to throw in the towel. Show me Lord the way of escape that you have provided for every situation that I may find myself in. And increase my passion for you so much that I would run to you in any situation whether good or bad. I love you and it is in Jesus name I pray, Amen.

We Overcome Autonomy:
My Thoughts

_____

_____

_____

_____

_____

_____

_____

_____

_____

_____

_____

_____

_____

I Am a Woman

I once knew a little girl without much to say.
I did not enjoy the presence of others, so alone I did play.
Not one sweet melody could come from my voice.
And the boys didn't like me, but that was my choice.

But because of my father's grace, when there is something to be
said, I raise my head and exalt my voice, so that all may hear.
And when one becomes separated from the rest of us, I tell
them that there is a friend in Jesus and draw them near.
At times, when I feel the urge for anger and
begin to raise my voice, I humble myself,
become scuttle and peacefully walk away.
As for those boys that didn't see anything in me
then, they can't help but notice my sweet soft
sway and the beauty that my soul portrays.

For I am a Woman, a Woman I Say I am.

There was once a young girl who didn't know how to smile.
I didn't have the clothes, shoes, or that rich girl profile.
Every one looked over and around this dark skinned child.
They said I was ugly, stupid, and couldn't be apart
of their group because my hair was wild.

But, because of my Jesus, I have a smile
that can stop a man in his tracks.
He will defiantly say there is something
special about her, and that's a fact.
And though I may not have those fancy
clothes and them hundred dollar shoes.
I have a spirit that allows me to always look good as I make do.
Oh YES, it has become real difficult to look over me now.
For I walk my walk and talk my talk, and will surely brighten
a room with my little light leaving others wondering how.
And though they may have said I was ugly,
stupid and couldn't be apart of their group,
It doesn't matter now because I belong to a much
higher cause who will not judge me with plain
sight, nor by the results of man's silly flukes.

For I am a Woman, a Woman I Say I am

PART TWO

We Overcome Abandonment

We Overcome Gossip

We Overcome Low Self-Esteem

We Overcome Rape

We Overcome Super Spirituality

We Overcome Hopelessness

We Overcome Physical Abuse

We Overcome Weariness

We Overcome Abandonment

And he that sent me is with me: the Father hath not left me alone; for I do always those things that please him.

John 8:29

I Am Torn

What have I done wrong to make you treat me this way?
All of my life I have only wanted to see
you smile to remove my dismay.
But, once again, today is not that day.
So I am frustrated because it's my young
heart you choose to slay.

What is it about them that permits you accept them and not me?
I feel like a begging dog that is crying
for love at your sorry knee.
But you act as though I don't even exist.
You smugly pushed me to the side to be
beaten by another man's fist.

I hate the fact that I was ever born.
And I hate all men even more.
I hope you are happy now that you have messed
up my life right along with yours.
And know that I will never accept you for
the years you chose to ignore.

My Sweet Child

Sometimes people don't do what they're suppose to.
Sometimes people make wrong choices, because
they don't think things through.
But that doesn't mean you can't be what you dream to be.
You are overflowing with many great things,
and you make me very happy.
You are so special that I gave you your
name before I made the Earth.
You are so precious that I gave you a purpose in
life before your mother ever gave birth.
So you see, your life was never based on the
mistakes that others choose to make.
And even though it hurt you, there's no real reason to hate.
So love them as I have loved you.
And let me deal with what they have put you through.

I Love You,
Daddy God

We Overcome Abandonment: Prayer

My Father, who is in heaven, I thank you for loving me the way you do. I want you to know you are my lifeline. Thank you for rescuing me. Thank you for never leaving as so many have. And, thank you for thinking and speaking good of me. You are a great friend, and I love you.

I will honestly admit that I have a whole in my heart where my loved one is suppose to be. It hurts so much to see other parents interact with their children. I begin to cry, because that is all I have ever wanted. I want it so bad that I have done crazy things to get my loved ones to notice me.

When I pray you tell me that you will fill this whole in my heart and replace it with you. I give you permission to heal me. Make it so that I will not feel desperate, or weak because of them. Give me a heart that is filled with happiness, peace, and love. And if there is anything I don't know to ask you for that I need please give it to me.

Thank you in advance. In the name of Jesus I pray, Amen.

We Overcome Abandonment: My Thoughts

We Overcome Gossip

A talebearer revealeth secrets: but he that is of a
faithful spirit concealeth the matter.

Proverbs 11:13

I'm Glad It's Not Me

That's the one.
That's the girl I told you about.

It's so sick.
She had her baby killed last month.

Look at her.
I wonder what her family said.

She don't care.
I heard her bragging about it.

Who's the Dad?
I heard that he goes to our school.

Nobody knows.
Everyone says she gets around.

Wow, Really?
She seems like a good girl to me.

Lets go now.
She knows were talking about her.

Can You Understand?

Is there anyone here that really cares?
She's broken, afraid, and hates life because it isn't fair.

Her stepfather sneaks into her room each night.
The walls close in around her as she's filled with fright.

He pridefully steals her innocence, and tells her to lie.
"If you tell anyone, your sister will surly die!"

So she tells her mother she is pregnant by someone at school.
Mother slaps her in the face, and calls her a garden tool.

And her very sister runs to tell everyone
that she had an abortion.
And here you are giving yourself false exaltation.

Now she walks the halls without a single friend.
Praying that someone would just try to understand.

Will it be you, or will you stay in the comfort of the crowd?
Thinking your "all that" with your head stuck in a cloud.

In case you didn't know, they will be lying about you next.
So I advise you show some maturity, and give her your respect.

We Overcome Gossip:
Prayer

Dear Heavenly Father I thank you for this day that you have created, and for allowing me to be in it. I thank you for loving me despite the things you see in me that don't please you. Lord I repent now for all the things I have done that has hurt you. Please forgive me in the name of Jesus.

One way that I now realized that I have hurt you is by gossiping. I see in Proverbs 11:13 that someone who is faithful to you would not hurt people by revealing their secrets. I am sorry Lord and I pray that you would remove that character defect from me.

I pray for the people whom have been hurt by the gossip I have spread. I pray that you would heal the many wounds in their hearts, and allow them to be stronger people because they have gone through this. I pray that you would give them a heart of forgiveness, and create a righteous relationship between us.

Thank you Lord, and it is in Jesus name I pray, Amen.

We Overcome Gossip:
My Thoughts

_____

_____

_____

_____

_____

_____

_____

_____

_____

_____

_____

_____

We Overcome Low Self-Esteem

Seeing then that we have a great high priest, that is passed into the heavens, Jesus the Son of God, let us hold fast our profession.

Hebrews 4:14

What's Wrong With Me?

Why does everything bad always happen to me?
I'm surrounded by people who seem to be so free.
What is their secret?
If they were selling it I'd buy it.
First my father doesn't want me; I am molested,
and beaten in one form or another daily.
Next my mother gives me away, and I fight
at school for being called ugly.
I am too skinny, and get teased for being too tall.
Honestly I'd rather not be seen or heard at all.
No one wants me, and I understand why.
I keep trying to take my life, but I just won't die.
I need a way out, and I crave something new.
Please God send someone to show me what to do.

This Is Who I Am

I am the righteousness of God, my father.
Everything I lay my hands on will prosper.
My estimated value is more than precious gems and metals.
I am intelligent, financially sharp, and
more beautiful than rose petals.
I choose to live, and not take my own life.
My life is running over with joy, hope,
and prosperity as Christ's wife.
I put God first, and follow his plan for me confidently.
I pray daily and expect my heavenly father to meet me.
Publicly and privately I speak with skill, wisdom, and kindness.
I humbly bless the poor with my portion of finances.
I diligently do all that that bible says I can.
And I am at the top when it comes to the matters of man.

We Overcome Low Self-Esteem: Prayer

Heavenly Father. I feel really bad right now. I wish I could put into words how I feel, but I would confuse myself trying to say it just right. Lord I am tired of hurting, and feeling less than everyone else. In Hebrews 4:14 you said to keep in my heart and speak with my mouth what you have said about me. And even though I sometimes don't believe I have the qualities you say I possess, I will be obedient to your commandment. I speak aloud what the bible says about me right now.

I am a child of the Most High God, and I hold a special place in His heart. Everything that belongs to God belongs to me. I am a leader and not a follower. I am at the top of all things, and not at the bottom being crushed. I can do all things through Christ because He gives me strength to do it. I have a life filled with hope, joy, and prosperity. Everywhere I go people want to bless me. My estimated value in the world is priceless. My spiritual cup overflows with God's love and abundance. Everything I place my hands on will richly succeed. And I am an overcomer because Christ has overcome the world.

Thank you Father for believing in me. I appreciate you and love you even more. It is in Jesus' name I pray. Amen.

We Overcome Low Self-Esteem: My Thoughts

_____

_____

_____

_____

_____

_____

_____

_____

_____

_____

_____

_____

_____

_____

We Overcome Rape

For whatsoever is born of God overcometh the world: and this is the victory that overcometh the world, even our faith.

1 John 5:4

There Won't Be a Next Time

He wants to talk; I wander what about.
I don't know him well, so trusting him is a doubt.

He is closing the door, and locking it too.
Good God what have I gotten myself into!

I can't believe what he just said.
Take off your clothes and get on the bed?

At school they tell us to do what they say.
Lord why is this going down this way?

Thank you God he is using protection.
I should have said no and pay attention.

Dude, what time is it?
Mom is going to have a crazy fit!

A minute in a half...felt like twenty years.
Okay, don't show your anger or fear.

Gross, he is stumbling as he turns back on the lights
Man, I just want to run away regardless of it being night.

I will go back in there, and pretend like nothing is wrong.
Dude, I hate myself for not fighting and
not saying anything this long!

I better not tell anyone since it is all my fault.
I should have looked for the signs or told him to halt.

I am never going anywhere else again.
And if I had my way I would castrate all men.

It Can't Be Taken

Devil you're a liar and you know you can't win.
It's just like you to use something as low as sexual sin.

I can admit it is a gamble that you win oftentimes.
But the bible tells me that you have to
pay me back every single dime.

I am not afraid of you, and I will never hide from you again.
Not another one of your tricks will I so easily befriend.

I will continue to fight you every step of the way.
There is nothing about me that you can ever steal away.

You will be so sorry now that I know who I am through Christ.
I can already see you trembling as I ask God for advice.

So be ready, because Christ has equipped
me to victoriously fight the war.
And I guarantee, with the fierceness of
the Lion, you will feel my roar.

We Overcome Rape:
Prayer

God, my true father, I thank you for loving me for who I am. Sometimes I don't understand how you can look at me as still see my purity as though I were just born. Lord, you are the only one I put my complete trust and confidence in. I love you so very much.

Father, sometimes it still hurts to think of how someone violated my body and I can be very cruel. I pray that you would allow me to forgive the person who has done this to me, and free my mind of it. I no longer want to live in yesterday. I want to live for today, and take advantage of the awesome future you have for me.

I pray that one day I would be able to use what has happened to me to help someone else. Please give me complete healing of my rape, and allow me to see that the devil has never had any victory over me.

I love you, and it's in Jesus name I pray. Amen.

We Overcome Rape:
My Thoughts

_____

_____

_____

_____

_____

_____

_____

_____

_____

_____

_____

_____

_____

We Overcome Super-Spirituality

Beware lest any man spoil you through philosophy
and vain deceit, after the tradition of men, after
the rudiments of the world, and not after Christ.

Colossians 2:8

I Choose to Listen to My Heart

My life has not always been easy, and I have
placed myself behind iron bars.
But yet I feel in my heart that God can
remove all of my bruises and scares.
I speak to other women of God who seem to
have joy and peace in serving Him.
But their response to me is that I will never
be on the same level as them.
They say it is because of my past, genealogy, and spiritual look.
But God showed me that He would even
use a donkey in His life filled book.
I've even been told that if I pray God would
choose not to hear my prayers.
And because I have no purpose of life, a
relationship with me God just wouldn't bare.
So my question now is, "Am I even saved"?
God promises to whoever would believe in His
son that their sins would be waived.
But according to these people that does not apply to me.
They believe that I am tainted, unusable, and send
of a foul odor before men and God almighty.
I don't know a whole lot about the things
of God, and what the bible says.
But my heart keeps telling me to keep after him,
and I won't give up until that changes.

They Were So Wrong

I thank God for giving me the ability to do anything.
I am grateful that he meets me when I pray and sing.
I have the pleasure of sitting before Him as
a small child who admires his father.
I enjoy the privilege of asking Him absolutely
anything, and He answers me as daughter.
I dream of the many great things He's promised I'd do.
I imagine the beauty in the places to which I will
travel as though the world were brand new.
I love how gentle He is with me, and how
He has made my self-worth priceless.
I appreciate Him for who He is, and place
Him above all earthly devices.
I know without a doubt I am as free as I
can be, and enjoy everyday life.
I say thank you Lord for healing my hurts, and
rescuing me from all my past and current strife.

Amen.

We Overcome Super-Spirituality: Prayer

Father of Heaven, I give you all glory, honor, and praise for my life. Thank you for this great work you have begun in me. I know that you are capable and willing to finish what you have started. Thank you Lord for the bible, which contains the truth about heavenly and earthly matters.

My prayer is that I would begin to read the bible more so that I can know your truth for myself. Lord I don't want to have to depend on other people to pray for me, or heal me. I want to be able to come to you on my own, and tell you everything in my heart.

I also ask Lord that you would show me what is my purpose in the Earth and equip me to fulfill it. The desire of my heart is to demonstrate my love for you by allowing you to use me. I want your supreme will in my life, and I thank you in advance for all you will do in me and through me.

In the name of Jesus I pray. Amen.

We Overcome Super-Spirituality:
My Thoughts

_____

_____

_____

_____

_____

_____

_____

_____

_____

_____

_____

_____

We Overcome Hopelessness

For we walk by faith, not by sight

2 Corinthians 5:7

How Much More Can I Take!

Can anyone tell me why it feels like the
world is weighing me down?
I see myself as a nail, and my surroundings as
a hammer driving me into the ground.
As soon as I rise above the odds there is
something there to slap me in the face.
It makes it easier to say daily that I truly hate this place.

I Know You Are Here

Sometimes this walk of life seems very tough. Deep
in my heart there is so much pain, but overshadowing
hope. Lord, I don't want to be a big talker or one who
can call a great bluff. I just want a constant peace of
mind for the challenges with which I must cope.

Sometimes I cry and wish that I had somewhere to run.
I become undesirably bitter, as my thoughts grow more
and more negative. Lord, I hear you telling me that
you are the only person I should depend on. I thank
you for cherishing me and for being so protective.

Sometimes I get discouraged and say things that I
shouldn't. I become as a balloon that has no more room
to receive air. Lord, I would like to be able to instantly
apply all of the instruction to my life that I see in the bible
each night. Help me apply your promises to my life, and
through them make my trials much easier to bear.

Sometimes I am very happy and my zeal can brighten a room.
I know you have shown me great favor in all that I do. Lord,
as a flower, you are what I need to bloom. I will continue
to worship you, and hope to one day be used by you.

We Overcome Hopelessness: Prayer

Father of heaven, I will always exalt your name. I appreciate all that you do in my life from day to day and moment to moment. You are more than enough, and all that I need.

Thank you for never giving up on me. I make so many mistakes and sometimes I loose the desire to keep on trying. In my heart I really don't want to give up. You have brought me too far to give up now.

I ask that you would give me everything I need to stay hopeful when things are not going my way. I realize Jesus lives inside of me, and I know that He is my reason for hope. As it says in 2 Corinthians 5:7, I choose to live by the measure of faith that you have given me, and will not be moved by my current situation. I give you all the praise in advance. In the name of Jesus I pray. Amen.

We Overcome Hopelessness:
My Thoughts

We Overcome Physical Abuse

He that troubleth his own house shall inherit the wind: and the fool shall be servant to the wise of heart.

Proverbs 11:29

Hands of Blood

Is this a dream?
Could this reality be what it seems?
I see a man, big in stature.
I see a woman, also, who he's trying to capture.
He corners her off in a small, small room.
She looks at him in fright, and wonders if this is her doom.

He whirls a towel, and demands that she put her back to him.
She looks at his hands and envisions blood on them.
Having complete faith in God, she turned around as told.
He placed the towel around her neck, which she began to hold.
Never once did she struggle, or put up a fight.
He continued to pull with all his might.

She obediently didn't give him the
satisfaction he was looking for.
So he let her go, and said, "I will love you forever more."
I see her lying in bed awake unable to rest.
She's thinking of what day her escape would be best.
This seems so real, so it can't be a dream.
I will pray for them both, and try not to scream.

A Mother's Prayer

Holy are you, my God,
Worthy is your name!
Holy are you, my God,
Throughout the world is your fame.

You are above the highest of mountains.
No beautiful site is more breath taking than you.
You are deeper than the greatest depth.
None on Earth can keep the promises you've kept.

My Lord, I am devoted to you.
My lover, my friend; daily you teach me something new.
You are wonderful for being simply who you are.
I thank you Lord for never being too far.

Amen.

We Overcome Physical Abuse: Prayer

Thank you Lord for always being here for me. I know you are here with me right now, and no one loves me more than you. You are so wonderful, and I am so glad you are apart of my life.

Father, it says in the bible that the devil is the king of lies, and his only mission is to steal, kill, and destroy the lives of the people you love. I hate that my loved one was influenced by the devil to perform physical abuse. It makes me so angry that the devil has stolen my innocence to physical abuse, killed the trust we once had, and destroyed our family.

I ask in Jesus name that you would forgive me for any unforgiveness I hold in my heart toward my loved one. And, allow me to forgive them for the hurt they have brought upon my family. I pray that you would set them free from the grasps of the devil, and allow them to forgive themselves for what they have done. Lord, you said in your bible that your mission is to bring abundant life to the ones you love. Please restore life to my loved one, and my life be better than it ever was before.

In Jesus name, amen.

We Overcome Physical Abuse:
My Thoughts

_____

_____

_____

_____

_____

_____

_____

_____

_____

_____

_____

_____

_____

We Overcome Weariness

But they that wait upon the LORD shall renew their strength; they shall mount up with wings as eagles; they shall run, and not be weary; and they shall walk, and not faint.

Isaiah 40:31

I Have No Fight Left

I don't understand why I feel this way. I am neither happy nor
sad, but just here. Does anyone understand what I am trying
to say? I am tired of fighting, and insanity is drawing near.

My body aches, and I am afraid to think. I am annoyed
by people, and cry about every little thing. I don't want
to eat, and I am loosing hope every time I blink. Lord
I feel that I am hanging on by a tearing string.

I want to give up on every thing, and I know I won't.
I pray to wake up tomorrow with a whole new zeal. I
am watching every thing of value rapidly demote. And
I fall helpless as my entire household becomes ill.

I don't feel as though I have displeased you Lord. In advance
I ask you to forgive me. If you don't help me I will be
permanently floored. Open my eyes that I may truly see.

Rise Up My Love

You are doing so well, and I am proud of you. The angels
are cheering with me as you press through. As the
rainbow, there really is a treasure on the other side. It is
a brand new land where my fulfilled promises abide.

Your enemy is desperate, and has saved his best for last.
He is hitting you hard, and his strategy is to do it fast.
This is why I have taught you patience and longsuffering.
I knew in the future this day would be coming.

So rise up and take your authority in me. You remind him
that he is messing with the daughter of the King. My word
is your fiercest weapon, and your shield will prove strong.
And he will remain under your feet where he belongs.

Once again I am very proud of you. Seeking me, Love, was the
right thing to do. I will be your strength, and your protection
too. And you will now have peace the rest of the way through.

We Overcome Weariness: Prayer

Sweet father of Heaven and Earth, I thank you for showing me that this season of my life will soon pass. I feel so much better knowing that I am not facing any of this alone. I am so thankful that you are always here for me, and for always keeping your promises.

Right now Lord I receive the peace and joy that you freely provide. I pray Lord that I would keep my eyes on you, and press toward the goals you have given me. May I use the measure of faith that you have given me at all times. And allow me to recognize the things that you do for me daily, so that I may not loose hope.

Thank you Lord for safety as I abide in your will. In Jesus name, amen.

We Overcome Weariness:
My Thoughts

_____

_____

_____

_____

_____

_____

_____

_____

_____

_____

_____

_____

_____

Someone...Mother

Someone is going to be there, mother, in your time of need,
To make sure you never want or have to plead

Someone is going to comfort you, mother, in your time of sorrow,
To help you today and promise a better tomorrow

Someone is going to love you, mother, even when you are at fault,
To keep you from becoming completely distraught

This big someone is only little me, and
forever at your side I'll always be

Someone is going to hold you up, mother, when you are down,
To up raise your spirits and get rid of the frown

Someone is going to have a shoulder, mother,
when you feel the need to cry,
To tell you loving and comforting words
no amount of money can buy

Someone is going to give you, mother, the time of day,
To encourage you when everything fails, and nothing goes your way

This big someone is only little me and
together, forever we'll always be!

Author's Note

Thank you for purchasing We Overcome All Things. You are on the great track to your complete recovery. It is important that you begin attending a good, bible-based church that will help you cultivate your growth process. If this book has helped you in any way I would love to hear from you. You may email your comments or testimonies to myjohnfd@msn.com or on Facebook at Author Myeisha Johnson. Thank you again for your purchase and God bless you.